Avoiding a Small Church Mentality

Avoiding a Small Church Mentality

Paul Flodquist

RESOURCE *Publications* • Eugene, Oregon

AVOIDING A SMALL CHURCH MENTALITY

Resource Publications
An Imprint of Wipf and Stock Publishers
199 W. 8th Ave., Suite 3
Eugene, OR 97401

www.wipfandstock.com

ISBN 13: 978-1-60899-430-4

Manufactured in the U.S.A.

Contents

Introduction

As students of scripture, we recognize that in God's economy, numerical growth in the church is not a sure indication of success. It is also true, however, that a small number of worshippers in church on Sunday is not automatically an indication of piety. Large churches can be faithful to the Gospel of Jesus Christ, just as small congregations can be faithful in fulfilling their unique role within the Kingdom of God.

In this brief essay, we will seek to discover some of the most common ways in which church leaders unintentionally limit the growth of their congregations. As a result of our study, we will learn to recognize that there is a great difference between a small church *mentality* and a small church *reality*. A small church mentality is to be avoided because it contradicts the teaching of Christ concerning the spreading power and influence of the gospel (Matthew 11:12; 13:31–32). In contrast, the reality of a small church is to be accepted as a distinct possibility within the sovereign rule of God—if it is not the result of human failure (1 Corinthians 3:7).

A small church mentality is a set of beliefs that inhibit the power of God's Spirit in a particular congregation. This happens in two ways. First, it prevents the spiritual needs of the people in its own congregation from being satisfied. Second, it blocks the church from reaching beyond the borders of its membership to meet the needs of the surrounding community.

It may be painful to acknowledge, but invariably a small church mentality is a failure of church leadership, not the laity. It is simply out of the scope of church members' responsibilities to take upon themselves the role of leadership authority.

Much as within secular enterprises, church leaders occupy the positions of greatest power and authority. They create the policies and make the decisions that determine success or failure. The buck stops with them.

It's hard to imagine any pastor or group of church leaders consciously setting policies and making decisions simply to maintain whatever level of attendance their congregation has already reached. This would go against the dynamic, life-affirming and missionary nature of the gospel.

So what causes the small church mentality to creep into leaders' thinking? We need to think about how church leaders unintentionally thwart their own stated desire to see the ministry of the gospel grow and prosper in their midst. The conclusions we reach may not be persuasive to everyone, but it is my hope that at least in some measure they may be convincing to some.

1

All Doctrine, All the Time

IDEALLY, THE PURSUIT OF PURITY IN DOCTRINE is an intense hunger to know the nature and character of our Lord. Such zeal for the truth is commended by God (Acts 17:11). A problem arises however, when the search for truth becomes prized for its own sake as an abstraction, rather than being sought after in humility within the context of human need. When this happens, we cease to speak the truth in love, and reduce scripture to a mere weapon or trophy.

To prevent this from occurring, in every sermon a pastor should strive to apply the biblical text to the needs of those who worship. As strange as it might sound, by this definition a sermon that only rests in the contemplation of divinity is unsuccessful. Although it may have succeeded in stirring the imagination of the hearers, it did not move their hearts toward action.

If we consider the foundational doctrines that underlie the Christian faith, it soon becomes apparent that nearly every belief concerning the nature of God and man can be viewed both theoretically and practically. Whether we focus our attention on the holiness of God, Christology, the sinfulness of man or the nature of the believer as redeemed in Christ, we can find plenty of material both for deep meditation as well as a wealth of information for living biblically every week of the year. These great scriptural themes provide everything that a pastor might need to counsel, rebuke and encourage his flock on how to live together in unity, and how to be witnesses to a lost and dying world.

When preparing a sermon, the minister of the gospel should not only ask, “What is the truth to be conveyed?” but also, “How should my listeners apply this truth?” Too often preachers take for granted that their hearers are relatively close in their understandings of the biblical text; worse, too often preachers take for granted that their hearers will make the leap, unguided, from truth to application. But even in the most well-taught and homogeneous congregations this is not necessarily the case.

Sermons that elaborate on Christian doctrine but never move beyond the theoretical are satisfying only the academic interests of those who are trained in theology and are familiar with the nuances of a particular biblical text as it relates to the overall witness of scripture. Laypeople are much less apt to be appreciative of how the parts fit within the whole. In the pews, the most immediate concern is relevance: What is the pastor going to say within the next half hour that will make a difference to my daily life? Successful preachers do not remain enraptured merely with the texts of scripture as it reveals the character and nature of God and our Savior. Instead, they make the Bible come alive in the life of the congregation, both in individuals and in the whole.

All this emphasis on the sermon assumes that the main draw for church attendance is the sermon. Many would disagree with this, pointing to studies that show the main reasons people choose to attend one church over another are things like social affinity, the style of music, and special programs.

I would suggest that while some studies might indicate the sermon is secondary, in Protestant worship services the sermon is central to the worship experience. This is because in Protestantism, explicating the Word of God (the Bible) became the main avenue of communication from God to His people, supplanting the preeminent place of the Mass in Roman Catholic services. Many other expressions of church life remain negotiable, but if the message from the pulpit consistently fails to satisfy, the people will look for secondary attractions elsewhere.

The term "felt needs" has come to be associated with excesses in the seeker-sensitive church movement in North America with its overemphasis on market research, consumer-oriented programs, compromised worship, superficiality in teaching and discipline, elevation of spiritually immature people to positions of spiritual authority, and obsession with supposedly bigger-as-better mega-churches. However, the idea of seeker-sensitivity itself is not necessarily bad. Jesus himself was very attuned to human need; many gospel stories revolve around very real and legitimate concerns. Clergy and theologically trained laypeople who feel disdain for the concept of felt needs may believe that theology must always have preeminence, or that it is unbiblical for laypeople to determine spiritual priorities and usurp the role of God-appointed church leaders. This attitude assumes that only those who possess formal theological training, or a call from a church to full-time pastoral ministry, have the necessary discernment to lead a church.

What leaders need above all is humility and a sense of balance. Clergy alone do not possess the Holy Spirit—or leadership gifts for that matter. Martin Luther talked about the priesthood of all believers; the New Testament itself says the Holy Spirit apportions spiritual gifts for the good of God's people as God wills (1 Corinthians 12:4–11). We see from scripture and Church history that the Holy Spirit has in the past, and reserves the right in the future, to reveal the appropriate needs of a particular faith community to laypeople, not only to the paid, full-time leadership. While this may not be the normal way in which God works, wise pastors will remain open to the experience.

Although it may seem counter-intuitive, a pastor can unknowingly indulge the carnality and spiritual immaturity of his congregation by putting too much focus upon doctrine, as if doctrine were an end in itself. When this happens, it can lead to a sectarianism that is content to remain isolated, rather than reaching out beyond its borders with the love of Christ to those who think differently.

2

Idiosyncratic Piety

Idiosyncratic can be "a peculiarity of constitution or temperament" as well as "an individualizing characteristic or quality."[1] The definition of piety is more familiar: "marked by or showing reverence for deity and devotion to divine worship."[2]

Piety becomes peculiar and individualistic according to the "doctrinal tone" of the congregation. The doctrinal tone is set by a particular subset of Christian beliefs or practices that have been selected and upon which the congregation is to be intensely focused. In turn, this subset of beliefs is determined not by church members, nor those in positions of lay leadership, but by the clergy alone.

In establishing the doctrinal tone of a congregation, the pastor is expected to operate within the framework of a denominational affiliation or faith tradition. Most denominations and faith traditions within Protestantism have, over time, developed polities that restrain peculiar or individualizing expressions of piety. But these systems aren't perfect. Denominational leaders can knowingly allow or neglect situations in which local congregations allow strange or out-of-balance theological beliefs to take root and flourish.

This means that the first line of defense against church leaders imposing regimes of idiosyncratic piety is the local church's lay leadership. If they are weak and unassertive, they give the pastor permission to assume the position of power without any accountability. If they also lack basic theological knowledge or the will to challenge the religious professional's realm of authority, they can easily be steamrolled. Therefore, it is essential for lay elders and those who serve on church boards to recognize that the spiritual authority God has given them in congregational matters is comparable to that of clergy; not less, but of a different type.

In other words, the Bible does not give leaders *carte blanche* to do whatever they want; living under the authority of scripture doesn't always mean "submitting to authority." When it's the responsible, right thing to do, the Bible portrays laypeople as taking moral stances against leaders and calling them to account. For example, when Saul, God's anointed king, made a foolish vow that would have ended the life of his son (and the hero of the battle) Jonathan, his soldiers rose up and did not allow him to carry out his vow (1 Samuel 14:24–28, 38–45). When the Jewish leaders demanded that the apostles stop preaching the gospel, the apostles refused to obey the ruling of the religious professionals (Acts 5:27–29). When charismatic leaders with idiosyncratic piety (and heresy) arose in the Early Church, laypeople were instructed not to welcome them or give them hospitality (2 John 9–11).

At what point, then, should laypeople today call a pastor with idiosyncratic piety to account? Here are some considerations.

The broad outline of the gospel accepted for four centuries by Protestant churches can be summarized in three "*solas*." *Sola Scriptura* (Latin for "scripture alone") establishes that the 66 books of the Old and New Testaments are the authoritative basis for Christian faith. *Solus Christus* (Latin for "Christ alone") states that Jesus is Savior and Lord, that he died for our sins and rose again from the dead, and that he will come again to judge the living and the dead. *Sola fide* (Latin for "faith alone") affirms that salvation is by God's grace through faith in Christ, as clearly declared in Ephesians 2:8–9.

So the first question lay leaders must ask is this: Does the pastor's personal agenda align or conflict with the broad outline of the gospel accepted for centuries by Protestant churches?

A second question must be: Does the pastor's personal agenda fit reasonably well with that of the denomination or faith tradition with which the church is affiliated, or does it depart radically? If it departs, then for the sake of integrity the church needs to start asking some hard questions about its future direction and affiliations.

A third question is: Has our own denomination moved so far from core Protestant beliefs that leaders in our own denomination are painting our pastor as idiosyncratic, or rebellious, or having a personal agenda—when in reality our pastor is defending those standards and attempting to establish relationships and possibly make alliances with other churches that affirm historic Protestant Christianity?

Both denominational and non-denominational churches can suffer if they fall into the trap of allowing their pastors' personal idiosyncrasies to set the doctrinal tone in their congregations. In non-denominational churches, however, two additional dynamics are at play. First, non-denominational pastors generally have more authority over the local congregation; there is less oversight and congregants are generally more deferential to pastoral authority. Second, pastors of non-denominational churches aren't little guys ("Davids") battling against gigantic, powerful, rich and unfaithful or wayward denominations ("Goliaths"). They're the big guys in their congregation. Because non-denominational pastors have a freer hand, laypeople must be that much more aware and assertive if the pastor's personal agenda starts getting bizarre or out of whack.

The doctrinal tone of a congregation is not just important from the standpoint of one particular congregation in one particular denomination; it is important because all Christian churches exist within a particular culture, both shaped by and reacting against it. Additionally, all congregations face the challenge of figuring out how to remain distinct from society while at the same time being relevant. The Great Commission given by our Lord to "make disciples of all nations" (Matthew 28:19–20) requires nothing less.

If a congregation gets too comfortable with culture, or craves the culture's applause and reinforcement, it might decide only to offer emotional support for the common difficulties of life and fail to bring a genuine gospel witness of confrontation against the culture. If this happens the church has become indistinguishable from the society in which it finds itself; it has become merely a social gathering of individuals who happen to speak of God in a theoretical sense.

Conversely, if a congregation becomes too "peculiar" and "individualizing," it will become like a fraternal organization, with a secret language and rituals known only to those initiated into its mysteries, alienating itself from the community and from any possibility of evangelistic effectiveness.

Therefore, genuine piety and relevance must go together. And yet, when the pastor—and by acting passively, the lay leadership of the church—allow the pastor's personal idiosyncrasies and proclivities to be confused with the demands of authentic holiness, they make the church's worship and community life incomprehensible to those outside of their flock. Genuine piety and relevance are also divorced when churches remove standards of orthodoxy and forms of worship from the life-giving stream of God's Spirit, redefining religious traditions or making up new ones that have, at best, a tangential or illusory foundation in scripture.

An example of idiosyncratic piety today is Exclusive Psalmody, the belief that only the Psalms are to be used as songs in congregational, public worship. Churches that adhere to this practice do so from the conviction that church worship must be shielded from any unbiblical innovation. Since any songs created since the Psalms were collected over 2,000 years ago are, by definition, postbiblical, exclusive psalmodists believe they must be "unbiblical." As with most examples of idiosyncratic piety, we cannot fault the stated intention (to remain true to Scripture), but we certainly can fault the interpretation.

Unfortunately, idiosyncratic piety invariably results in unwarranted restrictions of things God allows, a gross misunderstanding of who God is, and a badly misplaced zeal (Romans 10:2).

3

A One Man Show

MINISTRY IN SMALL CHURCHES can tend to revolve around the pastor, a single individual.[3] In order for a small church to grow numerically, it must be willing to move away from focusing on the ministry of a single person and to multiply its ministry through the recognition and releasing of the laity's spiritual gifts and talents. If we are to truly speak of local churches as *communities* of faith, we must expand our concept of leadership beyond that of paid, professional clergy.

Why is this so important? One big reason is that any social group is strongly associated with that group's spokesperson, platform speaker or visual leader. The bigger that person's role and the more that person is bathed in the spotlight, the more the group becomes an extension of that lone individual. A church with the pastor as the only visual leader runs the risk of becoming identified with one imperfect individual, rather than with the broader mission of the congregation. This emphasis on one person also contradicts the New Testament's emphasis on the idea that God gives some individuals to the church for the purpose of equipping God's people (the laypeople!) for the work of ministry (Ephesians 4:12). A more subtle reason is that the releasing of gifts and talents encourages worshipers to step out in faith, to take the initiative, and to break through the unfortunate human tendency to take the path of least resistance and simply follow the instructions of one strong leader. It also encourages them to better inform themselves about the beliefs of the group, rather than simply identify with personalities.

It is crucial for the overall life and vitality of a church to separate its identity entirely from pastoral leadership, whoever the paid professional pastor might be. To accomplish this, whenever possible, other members of the church should be allowed to become visible in the use of their unique gifts. This exercise of visual leadership is not merely so that their gifts can be recognized, but also so that the congregation's identity—both historically and in its present local manifestation—might transcend the role of the clergy. Employing and recognizing the gifts of the people strengthens the congregation's unique mission into the broader community by allowing the people in the congregation to forge many points of contact with the community.

We're talking about the "plurality of public leadership"—drawing back the curtain on the hidden wealth of talent in any congregation. As long as the congregation's talents are left unrecognized, or (more perniciously) squashed or squandered, its God-given leaders will remain untapped. Meanwhile, the conversation and thoughts of those in the pew will remain focused not upon the unique identity and mission of the congregation, but upon the personality and performance of the pastor, as if the congregation's job is to feed the pastor's ego.

Unfortunately, some pastors block church members from publicly exercising their spiritual gifts, imagining their involvement to be a threat to the integrity of their own ministry. A more common problem is a lack of willing participants. This hesitancy may come from previous negative experiences with pastoral leadership. However, a bigger problem is their pastors' inability to communicate their passion for ministry to others.

Why would pastors, who presumably are gifted in preaching and teaching, often be so singularly ineffective in motivating others? Some pastors possess only a lukewarm interest in motivating the members of their congregation in the area of public ministry because they are insecure about their post or unsure about their calling. Over time they have become very skillful at hiding their own doubts and projecting their insecurities onto others. Church members who unintentionally infringe upon the pastor's area of responsibility are quickly sidelined, ostensibly for the good of the congregation.

On the other hand, pastors of growing and vibrant faith communities gladly share responsibilities that can be done just as well, or better, with others. They understand that everything doesn't have to be done by them, and that they don't have to get all the credit. They also understand that even though activities and responsibilities can be transferred to others, this does not relieve them from their own position of being the responsible authority over everything that happens under their ministry; this "buck stops here" authority is not transferable to anyone else.

In other words, pastors must allow for people to learn from their mistakes. They need to create an environment in which their people can try different things and find those areas in which they really shine. This can feel very risky, especially for pastors who are risk-adverse.

But while pastors may worry about mistakes that occur under their watch, they also need to carefully consider their own behavior. Foolish behavior by clergy during worship services can lead to a clique-like, insular church. Members decide to remain in a congregation for a variety of reasons. If they have been members for a long time, they are much more willing to tolerate the spectacle of their pastor's imprudence than are visitors or regular attendees who might be contemplating becoming members of the congregation. Long-time church members also have invested a lot emotionally in the life of their congregation, so much so that they will resist leaving, and will only leave when there has been a significant change of circumstances in their lives or in the life of the congregation.

Visitors, on the other hand, have expectations on what constitutes appropriate behavior for those who preach and lead in worship and they don't want to be surprised by goofy or strange things. Such expectations vary according to the individual. But there is not so much variation so as to make any and all behavior acceptable. The people who minister in front of the congregation during the church service, whether paid clergy or church members exercising their gifts, need to realize that they are representing God. Because of this, a certain level of propriety and decorum is necessary.

Off-putting behavior can be sinful, or merely foolish. In small churches, because of the few number of people in attendance, pastors may feel an inappropriate level of intimacy with people in the congregation. They may even use the worship service to deliver informal and jocular comments. As harmless as this might seem, such expressions of familiarity are not conducive to worship because they unintentionally exclude visitors from full participation.

Jokes and overly-familiar comments aside, a more harmful attitude is still prevalent in certain congregations, even in this age of multi-cultural sensitivity. In some churches, pastors make remarks that are derogatory and misrepresent other races, ethnic groups, political figures or religious beliefs. Making those kinds of comments gives false witness to the gospel and is a sure-fire way to insure that visitors don't return (Deuteronomy 5:20; Revelation 5:9–10).

Such individual bias on the part of church leaders might very well be accepted by the members of their congregations or by those of the same denomination or faith tradition. However, such comments will not be accepted by those visiting from the outside. Likely they will create such aversion that offended visitors will become "anti-evangelists," if not of Christianity as a whole, then of the offending congregation and denomination.

How can we then explain the anomaly of large churches whose pastors exhibit foolish and maybe even sinful behavior, yet do not suffer any apparent loss in attendance? For better or worse, we cannot escape the fact that we humans are, to a significant degree, socially conditioned; bad behavior is more readily viewed as being acceptable or normal if it is viewed and tolerated by many people.

What about the social pressure to conform to racism, ethnic stereotypes, or political viewpoints in smaller churches? To be sure, the pressure is there as well, at least for long-term members. However, a visitor to a very small church will feel much less pressure to subsume his or her own personal convictions within the context of a tiny body of worshippers, a group whose style of worship exhibits a small, clannish, unattractive and ultimately unsuccessful mentality.

4

A Besieged Minority (We Are the People)

If we truly believe that pride is a sin, and therefore something to be avoided, then neither a large number of worshippers or a few is cause for self-congratulation. Jesus himself did not start a mega-church; his followers were few; he even preached sermons that discouraged the less faithful among his followers, causing the number of his disciples to diminish (Matthew 10:37–38, Luke 9:59–62).

Though they be dedicated, though they persevere in their tasks, and though they have relatively wonderful motives, ministers of the gospel do not have the perfect mind of Christ. They certainly cannot afford to go around congratulating themselves on the power of their rhetoric or the size of their congregations. And even pastors with larger congregations, if they are honest with themselves, know that their own motives are not perfectly pure, and that the words of their sermons do not perfectly reflect a zeal for the advancement of God's Kingdom.

Human pride can show up in the snare of doctrinal arrogance. If we present ourselves as having the only right doctrine, magnifying peripheral aspects of scriptural interpretations into iron-clad tests of orthodoxy, we succeed only in allowing our pride to create boundaries which the Holy Spirit will not honor. Unfortunately, despite the Protestant consensus on the three *solas,* many areas of doctrine are disputed; the difference between essential and non-essential is not always clear; and it is not always apparent when such non-essential matters have been elevated out of their proper place. Giving them the benefit of doubt, we might say that no pastor or congregation consciously seeks to distort the gospel or the overarching message of the Bible. However, distortion occurs when carnal human nature imagines it can take ownership of and control the truth, rather than focusing upon finding legitimate, scripturally mandated and clear roles of service in God's Kingdom.

We must remember that God alone knows truth perfectly. No particular congregation or denomination has a monopoly on God's truth; all these human interpretations are, to some extent, culturally-bound. All are subject to the correction of scripture, the best thinking of God's people through the centuries, and the illumination by the Holy Spirit over time. When a particular congregation, or even an entire denomination, comes to believe that it "owns" a better and more complete understanding of God's truth than all others, it has allowed pride to deceive it into thinking that their group alone owns the truth. What is thought to be owned, however, is certainly not the totality of the Gospel, but instead only what is perceived to be a correct interpretation of a narrow slice of doctrine. This false ownership is then transformed into a myopic focus for a distorted form of piety, a piety that views other Christians as suspect because they do not accept the interpretation of the particular doctrine in question.

When faced with rejection from other Christians, those who claim to own the whole truth have a choice: give up on their claim (impossible!), or retreat into a siege mentality. As lonely guardians of the truth, they believe that their zeal for truth will inevitably be unpopular in such an age of compromise and accommodation.4

Many Christian denominations and sects have been born from just such inflexibility and hubris. However, doctrinal purity alone is not helpful in establishing the genuine purity and identity of any particular congregation. Other factors must be considered. Today, it is heartening to find individual churches historically connected to sectarian groups wisely choosing to de-emphasize these kinds of idiosyncratic doctrines, forms of behavior and rituals. What good are they if they serve only to strengthen religious traditions, and do not contribute to our shared identity as Christians?

Often, the smaller a church is numerically, the more stubborn and inflexible is the piety of its members. While larger churches are confronting the challenges of how not to lose their identity by being assimilated into the broader culture, smaller churches are consumed with bickering about things like which songs to include in the hymnal.

Another impulse found in small church mentality congregations is performance-based piety. This manifests itself in a legalistic desire to define Christian faith in such narrow ways that division and discord inevitably results. If you don't measure up to the community of faith's peculiar standards, affection is withheld. In performance-based churches, because slight deviations in inward belief are suspect it becomes all the more imperative that all kinds of outward actions be put under the community's microscope.

I once attended an adult Bible study in which personal piety in the mundane matters of everyday life was being discussed. In exasperation, one person in the room suddenly exclaimed, "Are there any ______________ in this room!?" We can fill in the blank with Baptists, Methodists, Lutherans, Pentecostals, Presbyterians, or any other denomination or faith tradition that we care to name. Significantly, the question was not "Are there any Christians in this room?" The outraged questioner had come to identify true piety not with the Christian church in its various formulations, but specifically with that person's own faith tradition.

As with so many other areas of congregational life, the solution to the problem of schism and narrowing definitions of piety rests almost exclusively with the pastor, elders and other church leaders. In order to flourish as a congregation and move beyond a siege mentality, the church's leaders must determine what amount of diversity in both belief and behavior is acceptable biblically, rather than caving in to the culture's pressure, on the one hand, or else slavishly insisting on carnal religiosity. A humble desire to further God's Kingdom is far more important than maintaining our petty legalistic kingdoms.

5

From Family to Community

The New Testament uses the symbolism of a household and family to describe the nature of the Church (Galatians 6:10; Ephesians 2:19). In a smaller congregation, the level of intimacy enjoyed by its members can seem cozy and familial. However, too much inward focus—to the exclusion of the surrounding community—will fall short of fulfilling our Lord's command to make disciples of all nations.

With respect to the surrounding community, God calls Christians to evangelism and social service. We might call these activities "gathering in" and "reaching out"—as Jude 23 says, "snatching some from the fire" and "showing mercy."

Some churches thus focus upon rescuing individuals from a sinful culture and hell; others focus on finding points of contact and meeting physical needs. While healthy churches accomplish both tasks reasonably well, out of balance congregations favor one approach practically to the exclusion of the other. This may be a conscious or unconscious choice, conditioned by such factors as denominational heritage, the personality of the pastor, and the identity of a particular congregation.

For a reaching-out church, the challenge is to meet human needs and make the message of the gospel culturally relevant without sacrificing the evangelistic imperative or doctrinal purity. For a gathering-in congregation, the challenge is to preach the gospel of eternal salvation without falling into the trap of viewing society as so corrupt that it is irredeemable, or assuming that being utterly different from the society is the only true measure of piety.

However subtle these distinctions might seem, the ramifications for ministry can be tremendous. The first approach presupposes the positive aspects of culture based upon God's work of Common Grace in all peoples and cultures; the second approach concentrates largely upon the deleterious effects of the Fall (Adam and Eve's transgression) upon human nature.

Neither of these approaches are complete. And yet how to simultaneously affirm and balance both remains elusive. How can a congregation recognize that God is at work in a culture, while at the same time sift out the carnality and unbelief so thoroughly mixed in? (It's hard enough to do that in the church!) To uncritically accept the culture, or blithely ignore God's authoritative law in all aspects of life is to embrace small-church mindedness.

Thus, a congregation that has emphasized reaching out to the exclusion of gathering in may suffer from a lack of church growth or loss of members due to the neglect of people's real spiritual needs. Similarly, a congregation that has emphasized gathering in to the exclusion of reaching out may very well also suffer from a lack of church growth and loss of members due to the neglect of people's real physical needs. Both cases reveal the incompetence of clergy in failing to recognize the dual emphasis in scripture. The church is not about either approving everything in the culture as good, nor is it about rejecting everything in the culture as bad.

Just because a church is small is not a validation that it is doing God's will. Just because a church is large does not mean it has sought only to gain the approval of the culture instead of God.

But God wants his churches, of whatever size, to grow in their impact upon the world. Therefore, a smaller church that recognizes it needs to grow will make a mistake if it retrenches and seeks to focus upon its perceived strengths of doctrinal purity and distinctive piety. In the long run, this course of action can lead to a congregation's demise.

To survive, let alone grow, such a congregation will need to risk undergoing an uncomfortable and possibly wrenching series of changes. Religious traditions that get in the way of God's Kingdom will need to be dropped. The church will need to reform its corporate identity to allow for greater diversity in doctrine and piety. Strict conformity to minor matters of belief and practice, and approval based upon conformity to these standards, will need to be relaxed.

To accomplish these things will require listening and leadership skills. The pastoral staff will need to take the lead in moving the locus of judgment from denominational standards and religious traditions to the timeless standard of God's Word. This is easy enough to say, but hard to do, since it requires the pastor to see beyond the limitations of his own religious heritage, a step many ministers are unwilling to take. Yet until God's Shepherds can honestly recognize the errors and weaknesses within their own denomination or faith tradition, they will never be able to break free from traditions that cause their congregations to become stunted and ingrown.

We have spoken of the Reformation's foundational requirements for doctrinal purity in the three *solas;* now let us consider the Reformation's foundational requirements for ritual observance: Baptism and the Eucharist (or, the Lord's Supper). There are many different ways churches practice Baptism in the name of the Father, Son and Holy Spirit. Some baptize infants; others reserve baptism as only for those who have made a conscious decision to follow Christ. Some sprinkle water; others practice full immersion. Similarly there are many variations on how to do the Lord's Supper. Some have the Eucharist every Sunday; some only once a quarter or once a year. Some use bread and wine; others use crackers and grape juice. Some pass the elements through the aisles; some have everyone come to the front. Despite these minor differences, Christians can appreciate and value each other as one Body of Christ.

Once the foundational building blocks of doctrinal and ritual purity have been satisfied, the communal aspect of our faith naturally follows. We apply our experience of divine love within the Body of Christ by caring for church members in all kinds of practical and mundane ways. Then, beyond the church membership, we extend God's love for the community to the poor, sick and vulnerable. These acts of mercy and compassion delight the heart of our Lord.

Unfortunately, some churches neglect not only the broader community, but also their own members. The responsibility for this kind of massive failure must be borne by the pastor. No one else in the congregation preaches to the people assembled every week; no one else is at every church board meeting; no one else possesses the authority to initiate change on a broad scale. Contrary to what some ministers might believe, no behind-the-scenes power broker on the elder board or church council wields so much influence that it outweighs the power of the pulpit, from which the very Word of God is proclaimed.

Yet even the power of the pulpit is insufficient to motivate the congregation if the pastor's words are negated by his behavior. The pastor's success in leading the congregation beyond the comfortable confines of religious tradition will depend on the pastor's integrity: has he only talked about love, or has he convinced people of his love in practical and down-to-earth matters? To put it another way, the everyday challenges of life provide a proving ground where ministers of the gospel can either succeed or fail.

At the same time that the pastor must motivate church members to take positive actions toward their community, he must be sure to address underlying motives, too. It is very unlikely that church members will be successful in their attempts at outreach to the community if they go with a holier-than-thou attitude of judgmental superiority. Whether these kinds of thoughts are verbalized or remain unspoken, they will instantly be observed by the people receiving help and the whole effort will become a farce. In reality, judgmental superiority indicates an insecurity which allows for only halting and hesitant forays into the surrounding culture.

Turning to churches that want to gather in, why might those who are doctrinally pure and ethically sound in their own estimation risk inviting into their fellowship those whose beliefs and morals are corrupt? One good reason is that Jesus did it! Ultimately, the hope is that newcomers would eventually come to accept the truth in Jesus and find salvation. However, while leading people to Christ remains the underlying mission statement of many churches and denominations, some congregations are relatively successful and others are relatively unsuccessful. What makes the difference?

Churches that are more successful in gaining new members extend acceptance to people wherever they are in their spiritual journey. They trust in the operation of the Holy Spirit within the life of the individual over time. They don't demand uniformity of belief and conduct up front, before acceptance is granted.

Churches that are less successful expect behavioral change prior to doctrinal acceptance. They make people jump through many doctrinal and behavioral hoops. They act as if a person's acceptance into the Church is based upon the judgment of their particular faith community, rather than the operation of the Holy Spirit working in the person's life.

It is the pastor's responsibility, as the leader of the congregation, to combat such judgmentalism. The pastor must vigorously counter this wrong attitude wherever it crops up, whether it has been a long-standing malady in the church, or it flows from within the pastor's own psyche or Christian upbringing.

Let's be honest. The people in any congregation are not perfectly holy; they are all in process. In any given week they may be on track with their spiritual life or really hurting. People often come to church with mixed motives. To admit this should not be shocking or surprising. Given this scenario, we need to believe that every week the Holy Spirit is at work struggling within the hearts and minds of everyone in the congregation (James 4:5): giving them hope that God can use them; determination to put aside sinful and self-defeating attitudes and behaviors; and courage to overcome fear of sharing the love of Christ with those outside the "holy huddle."

6

Small by God's Design

Unfortunately, the ideas that whatever works is best and that bigger is better are deeply engrained in American culture. As a result, many have applied a "business model" for evaluating success and failure to the church. In this model, small means unsuccessful. We must be aware of this mindset in many who come to worship. Overcoming this perception of failure is a challenge that most leaders of small congregations are ill-equipped to address.

To meet this need, many books have been published on church growth strategies and techniques. Our primary interest here has been on how to prevent smaller churches from shrinking to even smaller sizes and helping them to start growing again. To that end, the final issue we'll look at is the first-impression problem for smaller churches. This first-impression problem relates to the universality of the gospel. The message of the gospel is intended to be universal in its scope, and is understood by the average person to be welcoming to everyone. However, suspicions might be triggered in visitors' minds upon entering a worship service with a tiny number of attendees.

In countering this first-impression problem, we must first affirm with steadfastness the value, worth, and equality of all individuals before God, whether male or female, of whatever class or ethnic group. Second, we must reject the idea that churches be evaluated and judged according to business models. Third, we must understand that the standards of God's Kingdom are often in opposition to those of the unbelieving world. Therefore, it is foolish and unwarranted to base the success of any ministry principally upon the number of those who come to worship on any given Sunday. The presence of the Holy Spirit does not depend upon the number of disciples, but upon hearts full of awe and worship.

In short, God calls pastors to maintain a prophetic witness to God's people and to the wider culture; pastors are to recognize the good and salutary in the surrounding culture as well as to condemn the insidious and harmful. Therefore, since worship is the place where people in community encounter the holiness of God, great care must be exercised to avoid compromise. But even doing everything right doesn't guarantee "success" as commonly measured. Consider the prophet Jeremiah. He had a long, faithful ministry, but he died in obscurity in a foreign land (Jeremiah 43:2). Just so, many of God's choice servants do not have big followings, garner few accolades, and receive little recognition in this life.

Unfortunately in our day many Protestant ministers find God's Word so pallid and ineffectual that they feel it necessary to pad their sermons with comedic routines. Regarding music presentations, they cannot seem to comprehend that any line of demarcation ought to be drawn between worship and entertainment. These failures have resulted in an increasing desacralization of the church service. The boundary between the holy and profane has been breached; the Body of Christ has increasingly become a mirror of culture, a shadow of its life-transforming identity.

Churches that seek to imbue their members with a deep sense of the sacred are not taking the fast track to greater numbers; they may very well experience greater challenges to achieving numerical growth. In fact, they may never rise above small or medium church status. In a culture given over to pleasure-seeking, smallness may indeed be the cost of faithful discipleship.

In the introduction to our study, we distinguished between a small church mentality and a small church reality. The first is the result of man's failure; the latter is a manifestation of divine wisdom. It is quite possible in the providence of God for the pastor to fulfill his office in a manner which receives the commendation of our Lord, and yet for the church to remain small in numbers. This does not mean that God loves small congregations less. The second and third chapters of the Book of Revelation teach us that each and every congregation of the Lord Jesus Christ is both unique and beloved in the sight of God.

In God's Kingdom, smaller congregations definitely have a unique and vital place. For one example, smaller churches can and do fill niches and meet needs that larger congregations can't see or be bothered with. For another, many of God's saints prefer a small congregation to the crush and hassle, anonymity of the individual, or the politics of a larger church. Smaller churches are not "wrong;" larger churches are not "right." There is room for both.

It's much like the analogy that the Apostle Paul made regarding Christ's Body (the Church). Just as many of the roles and tasks in the local church fulfilled by individuals may seem inconsequential, but in reality are of great importance in God's economy—so also small congregations fulfill vital roles and tasks within the mosaic of God's Kingdom (1Corinthians 12:22).

It has not been the purpose of this brief essay to suggest that the longing for intimate fellowship and zeal for doctrinal purity—which so often characterize numerically small congregations—are in any way unworthy goals. Rather, the purpose has been to show that when such noble attitudes and longings succumb to human pride, "smallness" ceases to refer primarily to numbers and becomes a damaging spiritual condition that is very hard to reverse. Only by facing down pride and through honest re-evaluation can pastors avoid a small church mentality.

If after much prayer and soul searching, the pastor of a numerically small congregation can say with confidence that he has avoided the attitudes and practices which restrict and discourage the power of the Holy Spirit, he can be assured that he will one day receive our Lord's commendation for a job well done (Matthew 25:23; 1 Thessalonians 2:4).

Endnotes

1. Merriam Webster Online Dictionary.
2. Merriam Webster Online Dictionary.
3. Proverbs 15:22; 24:6
4. Job 12:2.